Stand Out

2

Reading & Writing Challenge

Rob Jenkins • Staci Sabbagh Johnson

HEINLE
CENGAGE Learning

Australia • Brazil • Japan • Korea • Mexico • Singapore • Spain • United Kingdom • United States

HEINLE
CENGAGE Learning

Stand Out: Reading & Writing Challenge, Second Edition

Rob Jenkins, Staci Sabbagh Johnson

Publisher, Adult and Academic ESL: James W. Brown

Senior Acquisitions Editor: Sherrise Roehr

Director of Product Development: Anita Raducanu

Developmental Editor: Tom Jefferies

Editorial Assistant: Katherine Reilly

Director of Product Marketing: Amy Mabley

Senior Field Marketing Manager: Donna Lee Kennedy

Product Marketing Manager: Laura Needham

Senior Production Editor: Maryellen Killeen

Senior Manufacturing Coordinator: Mary Beth Hennebury

Photo Researcher: Melissa Goodrum

Project Manager: Tünde A. Dewey

Compositor: Pre-Press PMG

Cover Designer: Rotunda Design

Illustrators: Ray Medici
James Edwards, represented by Sheryl Beranbaum
Scott MacNeill

Library of Congress Control Number: 2006281897

ISBN-13: 978-1-4130-0722-0

ISBN-10: 1-4130-0722-8

Heinle
25 Thomson Place,
Boston, MA 02210
USA

Cengage Learning is a leading provider of customized learning solutions with office locations around the globe, including Singapore, the United Kingdom, Australia, Mexico, Brazil, and Japan. Locate your local office at: **international.cengage.com/region**

Cengage Learning products are represented in Canada by Nelson Education, Ltd.

Visit Heinle online at **elt.heinle.com**
Visit our corporate website at **cengage.com**

Printed in the United States of America
7 8 9 10 11 12 12 11

CONTENTS

Unit 4: Housing

Unit 5: Our Community

Unit 6: Health

Unit 7: Work, Work, Work

Unit 8: Goals and Lifelong Learning

APPENDIX

TO THE TEACHER

About *Stand Out: Standards-Based Learning*

The *Stand Out* series includes a five-level basal series for English language learners designed to facilitate active learning, while challenging students to build a nurturing and effective learning community.

About *Stand Out Reading & Writing Challenge*

Stand Out Reading & Writing Challenge was written to give students additional practice in vocabulary, reading, and writing, while focusing students' attention on life-skill content.

    Stand Out Reading & Writing Challenge is aligned with the basal series and is divided into eight distinct units, mirroring competency areas most useful to newcomers. These areas are outlined in CASAS assessment programs and different state model standards for adults.

    No prior content knowledge is required to use *Stand Out Reading & Writing Challenge*. However, students will need the skill background necessary for their particular level. The books can be used as a supplemental component to *Stand Out* or as a stand-alone text.

Philosophy of *Stand Out Reading & Writing Challenge*

Stand Out Reading & Writing Challenge is intended for English language learners who need more practice with vocabulary, reading, and writing than they are given in most basal texts. Each unit takes students from a life-skill activity to vocabulary and reading practice and eventually to a finished piece of writing with the philosophy that students learn best when actively engaged in activities that relate to their personal lives and move from what they already know to new information.

Organization of *Stand Out Reading & Writing Challenge*

Stand Out Reading & Writing Challenge challenges students to develop their vocabulary, reading, and writing skills through eight unique units. Each unit includes a mix of activity types and caters to students with different learning styles.

▶ **Life-Skill Activity** Each unit opens with a life-skill activity designed to activate students' prior knowledge about the topic and prepare them for the following activities.

▶ **Vocabulary** Students are introduced to vocabulary that they need to better understand the reading. They will go through a series of activities designed to make them more familiar with the vocabulary and how it will be used. The lower levels use a variety of pictures to demonstrate much of the vocabulary. The higher levels introduce dictionary skills to help students become more independent learners.

▶ **Life-Skill Readings** Students will prepare for the reading by assessing their own knowledge and by making predictions about what they will read. Following the reading, they will do a variety of comprehension activities as well as expansion activities designed to help them relate the reading to their own lives.

▶ **Writing Practice** Students read a writing model and work through a series of pre-writing activities designed to facilitate their writing process. Their final task is to compose an original writing based on the previous model. Through the series, students progress from writing simple sentences to producing to complex paragraphs, and finally multi-paragraph writings.

▶ **Editing** Students self-correct their own work and then share with peers for more suggestions. Students complete each unit by writing a final draft.

▶ **Community Challenge** Each unit ends with a challenge that requires students to complete a community task related to the life-skill topic from the competency area that they have just worked with.

ACKNOWLEDGMENTS

The author and publisher would like to thank the following reviewers:

Marti Estrin
Santa Rosa Junior College, Santa Rosa, CA

Lawrence Fish
Shorefront YM-YWHA English Learning Program, Brooklyn, NY

Kathleen Flynn
Glendale Community College, Glendale, CA

Kathleen Jimenez
Miami-Dade Community College, Miami, FL

Daniel Loos
Seattle Central Community College, Seattle, WA

Maiyra Redman
Miami-Dade Community College, Miami, FL

Eric Rosenberg
Bronx Community College, New York, NY

PHOTO CREDIT

Unit 3
Page 26: ©Christopher Idone/Creatas/PictureQuest

Unit 4
Page 42: ©Jeff Greenberg/Alamy
Page 45: ©Chad Ehlers/Alamy

Unit 5
Page 49: ©Chuck Place/Alamy

All *unlisted* images credit to: ©IndexOpen.com

UNIT 1

Everyday Life

▶ GETTING READY

 A Look at the picture of Kenji's class.

 B Answer the questions. Check (✔) the boxes.

1. Where is Kenji? ☐ in a classroom ☐ at home

2. Who is he talking to? ☐ Edgar ☐ Concepcion

3. What time is it? ☐ 3:15 ☐ 9:15

▶ READING CHALLENGE 1

A **Answer the questions.**

1. What is the name of your school? _____

2. What time do you usually go to school? _____

B **Read Kenji's student survey.**

Jackson Adult School Student Survey

PERSONAL INFORMATION

Student Name __Nakamura   Kenji__   Date of Birth __1/10/1988__
                  (Last)   (First)

Nationality __Japanese__   Age __18__

Current Address __8825 South Hampton, Los Angeles, CA 90002__

FAMILY

Marital Status: ☒ Single   ☐ Married   ☐ Divorced   ☐ Widow(er)

Do you live with your parents? __Yes__   How many brothers and sisters do you have? __3__

Do you have children? __No__   How many children do you have? _____

Family members living in the U.S. but not in your home __uncles and aunts__

Family members living outside the U.S. __grandparents__

EDUCATIONAL GOALS	HOBBIES
☒ college ☐ university ☐ trade school ☐ other: _____	What do you like to do outside of class? Visit with my aunts and uncles

C **Complete the paragraph about Kenji.**

My name is Kenji Nakamura. I am from _____.

I am single. I live with my parents in the city of _____. I have

_____ brothers and sisters. I am tall and average weight. I go to

Jackson _____. My class is at 10:00 A.M. I want to learn English and

then go to _____ to improve my education. I like to visit with my

_____.

2 **UNIT 1 ● Reading Challenge 1**

A Learn new words.

He is *tall*.
She is *short*.

Mary is *thin*.
Victor is *heavy*.

He is *handsome*.
She is *beautiful*.

Steve is *bald*.

Maria is *shy*.

Ahmed is *smart*.

They are *talkative*.

Mario is *friendly*.

Dalva is *hardworking*.

Amal is *happy*.

He is *nervous*.

She feels *tired*.

B Words that describe people are called *adjectives*. Complete the chart with adjectives from Exercise A.

Adjectives of appearance	Adjectives of personality	Adjectives of feeling
short	*talkative*	*tired*

C Study the chart.

I	am	short.
You We They	are	tall. talkative. friendly. bald.
He She It	is	

Describe the people in the picture. Use adjectives and write sentences.

1. *Julio is average height. He is handsome.* _____

2. _____

3. _____

4. _____

5. _____

6. _____

D **Write sentences about people in your class.**

1. _____Larissa_____ is tall.

2. _____ is short.

3. _____ is friendly.

4. _____ is talkative.

5. _____ is average weight.

6. _____

7. _____

8. _____

E **Answer the questions.**

1. Is your hair blond? _____No, it isn't._____

2. Is your hair short? _____

3. Are you tall? _____

4. Is your teacher bald? _____

5. Are your classmates friendly? _____

6. Are you tired? _____

F **Make an "adjective" page in your notebook. Write the adjectives from this unit in your book.**

Adjectives

short
talkative

► **PRE-READING**

 A **You will read about Kenji. What do you already know?**

1. What is Kenji's last name? _____

2. Where is he from? _____

3. Where does he live now? _____

4. Does Kenji live with his parents? _____

B **Kenji's family is important to him. Look at Kenji.**

C **What do you think Kenji's family does together? Check (✔) the boxes.**

☐ plays games

☐ goes to restaurants for dinner

☐ goes to church

☐ watches television

☐ talks about Japan

☐ calls family in Japan

☐ studies English

☐ works in a restaurant

▶ READING

D **Read about Kenji.**

Kenji and His Family

   Kenji Nakamura lives in Los Angeles. He studies at Jackson Adult School. He is from Tokyo, Japan. Kenji is 18 years old. He is average height and thin. He has black hair. His mother says he is very handsome. ◀──── Paragraph 1

   Kenji lives with his parents, his sister, and his two brothers. He likes being with his family. His family is important to him. On Sunday, his aunt visits from Providence. She is very friendly. They eat breakfast together and go for a walk in the park. After the walk, ◀──── Paragraph 2
they call Kenji's grandparents. His grandparents live in Japan. Everyone takes a turn and talks. Kenji's grandfather is very talkative. Later, the family plays games together. Kenji likes the United States but is sad sometimes because his grandparents are not here with him.

▶ MAIN IDEAS

E **Each paragraph has a different idea. Write the number of the paragraph.**

Paragraph number	Main idea
	Information about Kenji's family
	Information about Kenji

► DETAILS

 F **Answer the questions.**

1. Does Kenji live in San Francisco? _____

2. Does Kenji have two brothers? _____

3. Does his aunt visit him on Sunday? _____

4. Does Kenji play games with his family? _____

5. Do Kenji's grandparents walk in the park with Kenji? _____

6. Does Kenji like living in the United States? _____

► EXTENSION

G **What do you do with your family? Check (✔) the boxes.**

☐ play games

☐ watch television

☐ talk on the phone

☐ eat meals together

☐ other: _____

H **Ask four classmates these questions. Complete the chart.**

1. Do you play games with your family?
2. Do you watch television?
3. Do you talk on the phone with your family?
4. Do you eat meals together?

Name	Question 1	Question 2	Question 3	Question 4
Kenji	✓	✗	✓	✓

► WRITING CHALLENGE

► PREPARING

 A **Read about Irina.**

My Family

January 15, 2006

By Irina Balack

My name is Irina Balack. I'm from Russia. I have a beautiful family. I am married and have a little girl called Larissa. Larissa is beautiful and very talkative. My husband's name is Alexi. He works in New York City. He's handsome. I am happy that I am in the United States with my family.

B **Complete the survey about you.**

_____ Student Survey

PERSONAL INFORMATION

Student Name _____ (Last) _____ (First) _____   Date of Birth _____

Nationality _____   Age _____

Current Address _____

FAMILY

Marital Status: ☐ Single   ☐ Married   ☐ Divorced   ☐ Widow(er)

Do you live with your parents? _____   How many brothers and sisters do you have? _____

Do you have children? _____   How many children do you have? _____

Family members living in the U.S. but not in your home _____

Family members living outside the U.S. _____

C Which adjectives describe you? Check (✔) the boxes.

☐ short   ☐ shy

☐ tall   ☐ happy

☐ smart   ☐ hardworking

☐ friendly   ☐ thin

☐ bald   ☐ talkative

D Write sentences about yourself.

1. [Your name] _____

2. [Where you are from] _____

3. [Your appearance] _____

4. [Your personality] _____

E Write sentences about your family. Use the information from the form on page 9.

1. _____

2. _____

3. _____

4. _____

▶ **WRITING**

F Write about yourself.

	About Me	

Write about your family.

	About My Family	

▶ **EDITING**

Check your writing.

☐ Capital letters: My name is James. ~~my~~ name is ~~james~~.

☐ Periods: I am from Argentina.

Check a partner's writing.

☐ Capital letters: My name is James. ~~my~~ name is ~~james~~.

☐ Periods: I am from Argentina.

J **Rewrite your paragraphs on another sheet of paper.**

A **Interview a neighbor and complete the form.**

Student Survey

PERSONAL INFORMATION

Student Name _____ Date of Birth _____
            (Last)   (First)

Nationality _____ Age _____

Current Address _____

FAMILY

Marital Status: ☐ Single   ☐ Married   ☐ Divorced   ☐ Widow(er)

Do you live with your parents? _____   How many brothers and sisters do you have? _____

Do you have children? _____   How many children do you have? _____

Family members living in the U.S. but not in your home _____

Family members living outside the U.S. _____

EDUCATIONAL GOALS

☐ college   ☐ university   ☐ trade school

☐ other: _____

HOBBIES

What do you like to do outside of class?

_____

B **Report your findings to your class.**

UNIT 2

Let's Go Shopping

 A Look at the picture of Lien's shop.

B Answer the questions.

1. Where is Lien? _____

2. What is the name of the store? _____

3. Does the store sell men's clothes? _____

A **Answer the questions.**

1. Where do you shop for clothes? _____

2. Do you buy cheap clothes or expensive clothes? _____

B **Read about Lien's Store.**

Danh Tù Women's Clothing

SALE THIS WEEK!

Prices start at $20

Prices start at $12

20% OFF REGULAR PRICE!

575 W. Main Street

C **Complete the paragraph about Lien and her store.**

My name is Lien Nguyen. I have a shop downtown. I sell _____ clothing.

I have a sale _____ week. Everything is _____ off the regular price.

I make my own dresses and skirts so they are very cheap. The price of _____

starts at $20. The price of skirts starts at $_____. Please come to my store and

visit me!

A **Study the words.**

The ***regular price*** is $25.
The ***sales price*** is $15.

The ***customer*** wants to buy shoes.
The ***salesperson*** helped Ivan buy new shoes.

There's a ***sale*** on sneakers.
You can ***save*** $5 on sneakers.

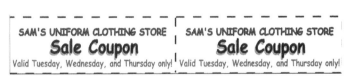

The shirts are $4 off with a ***coupon***.

Receipt		
Shirts 2@ $17.98	$	35.96
Sneakers	$	22.99
Tax	$	4.72
Total	$	63.67

The ***sales tax*** is $4.72.
The ***total*** with tax is $63.67.

I try clothes on in the ***fitting room***.

B Complete the sentences with words from the box.

employees	sale	coupon	regular	sales tax	total

1. There is a _____ on women's shoes today.

2. The _____ helped me find the right shirt.

3. The price for one pair of pants is $29.

   The _____ for three pairs is $87.

4. The _____ in my state is 8 percent.

5. The _____ price for blouses is $25 every day.

6. The sale price is $35, but you need a _____.

C *Conjunctions* are words that connect two sentences together. Use *because* to answer the question "Why?" Study the chart.

Because	
I like Sam's Clothing Store.	The prices are good.
I like Sam's Clothing Store **because** the prices are good.	
I go to Discount Market.	I like the salespeople.
I go to Discount Market **because** I like the salespeople.	

Read the statements. Use them to make sentences with *because*.

1. I shop at Lanstrom's Clothes.   Men's shirts are on sale every week.
2. I go to Barrel Boutique.   Their prices are usually very good.
3. I buy fruit at Save Now Market.   The regular prices are always low.
4. I prefer the Discount Books.   You can save money on books.
5. I shop at Boulder Books.   The salespeople are friendly.
6. I prefer Nickel's Department Store.   They have large fitting rooms.
7. I buy earrings at Jewelry A-Z.   They don't charge sales tax.

1. *I shop at Lanstrom's Clothes because men's shirts are on sale every week.*

2. _____

3. _____

4. _____

5. _____

6. _____

7. _____

D *Nouns* are people, places, and things. Complete the chart with words from the box. Add more words.

| coupon | blouse | sale | fitting room | receipt |
| salesperson | mall | customer | shorts | suit |

People	Places	Things
Lien	store	shirt

 E Use five of the nouns from Exercise D to write a conversation.

Customer: _Excuse me, can you help me?_____

Salesperson: _____

Customer: _____

Salesperson: _____

Customer: _____

Salesperson: _____

Customer: _____

Salesperson: _____

Customer: _____

Salesperson: _____

Customer: _____

F Practice the conversation with a partner.

G Make a "noun" page in your notebook. Write the nouns from this unit in your book. Look up the words below in a dictionary and add them to your notebook, too.

| discount | special offer | clerk | customer service |

► **PRE-READING**

A You will read about Lien. Look again at Lien's store. Make a list of clothes you can buy at Lien's store.

_____

_____

_____

B Lien's store is called Danh Tù. *Danh tù* is a Vietnamese word. Look at the picture. What do you think *danh tù* is?

☐ her father's name

☐ a flower

☐ where she was born

☐ a dress

☐ fashion

C **Read about Lien's store.**

Flowers from Home

Lien has a clothing store in Northern California called Danh Tù. The regular prices at the store are very good because Lien makes some of the clothes herself. For example, women's dresses are $15 to $30 before tax. She makes unique clothes. All her clothes are <u>different</u> colors and styles. Customers can try the clothes on in the fitting room. Lien has a new sale every week. She works every day except Sunday.

Lien also grows flowers in her store. The flowers help Lien remember her garden in Vietnam. Lien's favorite flower is the <u>orchid</u>. There are many orchids in Vietnam. *Danh tù* means orchid in Vietnamese. Lien is happy in the United States because she keeps part of Vietnam with her every day.

► MAIN IDEAS

D **Each paragraph has a different idea. Write the number of the paragraph.**

Paragraph number	Main idea
	Information about the clothing store
	Information about why Lien grows flowers

▶ DETAILS

 E **Answer the questions. Circle *True* or *False*.**

1. Lien sells clothes.	True	False
2. Lien doesn't make clothes.	True	False
3. Women's dresses cost $15 to $30.	True	False
4. The store has a new sale every day.	True	False
5. Lien works every day.	True	False
6. She grows flowers in her store.	True	False
7. *Danh Tù* is a name for a blouse.	True	False

F **Lien says she has "part of Vietnam with her every day." Why does she say this?**

1. Because she gets letters from Vietnam.
2. Because the flowers help her remember Vietnam.
3. Because her sister works with her.

G **Answer the question.**

She makes **unique** clothes. All her clothes are different colors and styles.
Unique means:

1. cheap   2. different   3. old   4. one

▶ EXTENSION

 H **Ask four classmates these questions. Complete the chart.**

1. Where are you from?
2. What do you have that helps you remember your country?

Name	Question 1	Question 2	Question 3

WRITING CHALLENGE

▶ **PREPARING**

A Read about Toots and Fruits.

> ### Toots and Fruits Toy Factory
> #### February 2, 2006
> #### By Nathan Zurry
>
> Toots and Fruits Toy Factory is a wonderful store. It is in Placentia, California. I like it because they have toys for young people and for older people like me. There is usually a sale. The salespeople are always very friendly. It is different because you can play with any toy before you buy it.

B Why does Nathan like the store? Write three reasons.

1. _____

2. _____

3. _____

C Complete the chart.

Clothing stores I like	
Food stores I like	
Department stores I like	
Other stores I like	

D **Choose your favorite store.**

_____

 E **Answer the questions.**

1. What does your favorite store sell?

_____

2. Where is it?

_____

3. Is it a big or small store?

_____

F **Complete the sentences about your favorite store.**

1. I like _____.

2. I like it because _____.

3. The employees are _____.

4. It's different because it has _____.

G **Look at how Nathan formatted his paragraph.**

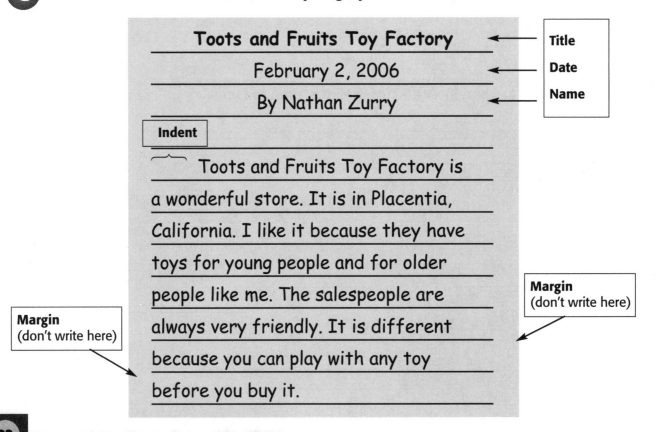

Toots and Fruits Toy Factory ← Title

February 2, 2006 ← Date

By Nathan Zurry ← Name

Indent

    Toots and Fruits Toy Factory is a wonderful store. It is in Placentia, California. I like it because they have toys for young people and for older people like me. The salespeople are always very friendly. It is different because you can play with any toy before you buy it.

Margin (don't write here)

Margin (don't write here)

► **WRITING**

H Write a paragraph about your favorite store.

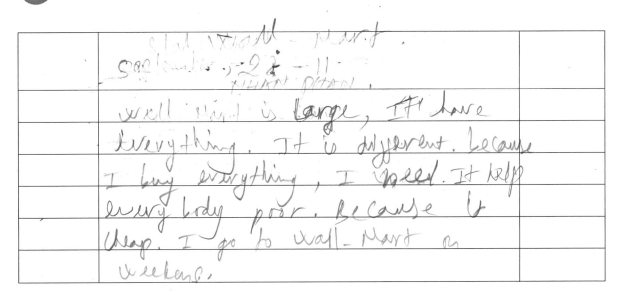

► **EDITING**

I Check your writing.

☐ Capital letters: (M)y name is (J)ames. ~~my~~ name is ~~j~~ames.

☐ Periods: I am from Argentina.

☐ Indent:

☐ Title, date, name

☐ Margins

J Check a partner's writing.

☐ Capital letters: (M)y name is (J)ames. ~~my~~ name is ~~j~~ames.

☐ Periods: I am from Argentina.

☐ Indent:

☐ Title, date, name

☐ Margins

K Rewrite your paragraph on another sheet of paper.

A Do a community survey. Choose five stores from your neighborhood. Make five copies of the survey. Talk to five people about their opinions.

Store Survey

Instructions: Please answer the questions honestly and anonymously. This is a class project and the information will not be used for other purposes.

Store name	Service			Employee attitude			What is unique?
	Good	OK	Poor	Good	OK	Poor	

B Report your findings to your class.

UNIT 3

Food and Nutrition

▶ GETTING READY

 A Look at the picture of Gilberto.

B Answer the questions.

1. What is Gilberto's job?

_____

2. What is he making?

_____

READING CHALLENGE 1

 Answer the questions.

1. What is your favorite food?

_____

2. Do you have a favorite recipe?

_____

B **Look at the recipe below.**

Feijoada *Serves: 8*

Ingredients:
1 pound beans, ¾ pound pork shoulder, 6 ounces of bacon,
½ lb pork sausage, ½ pound hot portuguese sausage,
2 pounds ham, 2 large yellow onions, 3 garlic cloves,
6 green onions, ½ tablespoon chopped parsley, 2 bay leaves,
1½ tablespoon oregano, chopped cilantro, salt and pepper.

Instructions:
Prepare beans. Soak beans overnight and drain. Cook in water
at low heat in a covered pot for 2½ hours or until almost
soft. Prepare meat Cook the sausages for 35-40 minutes.
Cook all other meat for 45-60 minutes. Add the meats
and juices to the beans. Add all seasonings. Simmer for
30 minutes. Serve on white rice.

C **Complete the paragraph.**

   Gilberto Moraẽs is a chef. He is from Brazil. He likes to cook feijoada. You need many

ingredients to make feijoada for _____ people. For example, you need one

pound of _____, six _____ of bacon, two _____ of

ham, 3 _____, and 1½ _____ of oregano. Cooking the beans is

difficult. The beans should be cooked for _____ hours. Gilberto is a good cook

and has a lot of experience, so his feijoada tastes great.

A Study the vocabulary.

A **_tablespoon_** is bigger than a **_teaspoon_**.

We need a **_pound_** of rice.

You need one **_cup_** of sugar to make the cake delicious.

Mix the ingredients well.

Boil water before you add the potatoes.

Add potatoes to hot water.

Chop the potatoes.

Cook on the stove for 20 minutes.

Peel the potatoes.

Honey tastes **_sweet_**. These peanuts are **_salty_**.

Jalapeños make food **_hot_** or **_spicy_**.

That cake looks **_delicious_**!

B *Taste* **is the feeling you have in your mouth when you eat or drink something. Some things taste good to you and some things taste bad. Describe the taste of the foods in the box. Complete the chart.**

apple	chips	noodles	burger	burritos	candy	soda	oranges
steak	fajitas	curry	stir fry	chocolate	jalapeños	french fries	

Sweet	Salty	Hot/Spicy
apple	*chips*	*jalapeños*

C **What foods do you think are delicious?**

_____

_____

D *Disgusting* **is the opposite of** *delicious.* **What foods do you think are disgusting?**

_____

_____

E *Verbs* **are often action words. There is always at least one verb in a sentence. Read the recipe and circle the verbs.**

<u>Mashed potatoes</u>   Serves 6

Ingredients: 6 potatoes, 2 tablespoons of
butter or margarine, 1 teaspoon of salt, garlic salt
to taste, 1/4 cup of milk. **Instructions:** Peel and chop
potatoes. Boil water. Add potatoes to boiling water.
Cook for 10 minutes. Drain. Mix all ingredients.
Whip with a whisk or a blender.

F Look at the picture. Complete the chart.

Peel	Chop	Boil
potatoes	apples	broccoli

G Match a verb to an ingredient.

_____ 1. the chicken into small pieces.   a. Add

_____ 2. two teaspoons of salt.   b. Mix

_____ 3. for 30 minutes at 250°F.   c. Boil

_____ 4. the carrots.   d. Chop

_____ 5. the ingredients in a bowl.   e. Peel

_____ 6. the water.   f. Cook

H Make a verb page in your notebook. Write the verbs from this unit in your book. Look up the words below in a dictionary and add them to your notebook, too.

simmer	fry	drain	whisk

▶ **PRE-READING**

 A Look at the pictures. What would you like to eat?

 B What do people eat in your country? Make a list of some foods from your country.

_____

_____

_____

C You are going to read about Gilberto. What do you already know?

1. What is Gilberto's last name? _____

2. Where is he from? _____

3. What is his job? _____

4. What does he cook? _____

D **Read about Gilberto's favorite dish.**

A Favorite Dish

Gilberto is from Brazil. He has worked at his father's restaurant for 10 years, but wants to be a chef in his own restaurant. He wants to share dishes from his country with the community. Gilberto wants to open a *churrascaria*—a Brazilian barbeque.

Brazil has some unique dishes. However, Brazilian food usually includes rice and beans. Some dishes are spicy, but most are mild. Almost every Brazilian recipe uses meat. Many Brazilians eat beef, pork, fish, and poultry.

Gilberto's favorite dish is a Brazilian stew called *Feijoada*. The name feijoada comes from the Portuguese word feijaõ. Feijaõ means beans. feijoada is a dish made with black beans and pork. Feijoada has many cuts of pork in it including bacon, ham, and sausage. Sometimes people eat feijoada with a very hot sauce called molho carioca. Gilberto will cook every kind of meat in his churrascaria, and feijoada will be one special dish.

poultry gia cans

► **MAIN IDEAS**

E **Each paragraph has a different idea. Write the number of the paragraph.**

Paragraph number	Main idea
	About *feijoada*
	About Brazilian food
	About Gilberto

► **DETAILS**

F **Gilberto wants to share foods from his country with the community. What does he mean? Check (✓) the correct answer.**

☐ 1. He wants people to know about Brazilian food.

☐ 2. He wants people to eat at his restaurant so he can make money.

☐ 3. He wants help in his restaurant making special foods from Brazil.

G Answer the question.

1. How long has Gilberto worked at his father's restaurant? _____

2. What three ingredients are in most Brazilian dishes? _____

3. What does feijaõ mean? _____

4. What ingredients are in feijoada? _____

_____

_____

H Match each word with its definition.

___c___ 1. a chef   a. has

___b___ 2. however   b. but

___d___ 3. dish   c. an experienced cook

___a___ 4. includes   d. a meal or recipe

▶ EXTENSION

I Ask four classmates these questions. Complete the chart.

1. What is your favorite dish from your country?
2. What are the main ingredients?
3. Do you know how to cook your favorite dish?

Name	Question 1	Question 2	Question 3

▶ WRITING CHALLENGE

▶ PREPARING

A Read about Alberto's favorite dish.

> ### My Favorite Dish
>
> #### March 22, 2006
>
> #### By Alberto Valenzuela
>
> The food in my country is delicious. I'm from Michoacan, Mexico. We eat a lot of rice and beans and we have many special dishes. I like hot sauce and jalapeño chilies on everything. I eat jalapeños for breakfast, lunch, and dinner. My favorite dish is Pollo Placero. Pollo Placero is chicken, vegetables, and enchilada sauce. We cook all the ingredients early, and then we heat them up again in oil.

B Make a list of four dishes you like.

1. _____
2. _____
3. _____
4. _____

C What is your favorite dish from your country?

_____

D Choose the words that best describe your favorite dish.

☐ salty   ☐ hot or spicy   ☐ Other: _____

☐ sweet   ☐ delicious

E **Use your choices from Exercises C and D and write a sentence.**

EXAMPLE: <u>*My favorite dish is curry. It is delicious and spicy.*</u>

_____

_____

F **Write the ingredients for your favorite dish.**

_____

_____

_____

G **How do you make your favorite dish? Write sentences using the words from the box.**

cook	boil	chop	peel	add	mix

_____

_____

_____

_____

H **Complete the answers.**

1. What is the food like in your native country, city, or town?

   We have a lot of _____

2. What do you like on your food? (For example: salt, pepper, hot sauce, Kim chi, etc.)

   I like _____ on my food.

3. When do you use it? (breakfast, lunch, or dinner)

   I use it for _____

4. What do you put it on?

   I put it on _____

► WRITING

I Write a paragraph about your favorite dish.

► EDITING

J Check your writing.

☐ Capital letters: My name is James. my name is james.

☐ Periods: I am from Argentina.

☐ Indent:

☐ Title, date, name

☐ Margins

Check a partner's writing.

☐ Capital letters: (M)y name is (J)ames. ~~my~~ name is ̷james.

☐ Periods: I am from Argentina◌

☐ Indent: ⁓

☐ Title, date, name

☐ Margins

 Rewrite your paragraph on another sheet of paper.

▶ Community Challenge

 Go out in the community and find recipes from your neighbors. Write them down.

B **Make a recipe book as a class. Make the dishes and bring them to school for students to try.**

UNIT 4   Housing

▶ GETTING READY

 A   **Look at the picture of Kyung and his family.**

 B   **Answer the questions.**

1. How many people are in Kyung's family?

   _____

2. Where do they live now?

   _____

3. What kind of home would be good for Kyung and his family? Why?

   _____

A **Answer the questions. Check (✔) the boxes.**

1. What kind of home do you live in?

   ☐ a house   ☐ an apartment   ☐ a condominium   ☐ (Other) _____

2. How many bedrooms do you have?

   ☐ 1   ☐ 2   ☐ 3   ☐ 4   ☐ Other

B **Read the housing ad.**

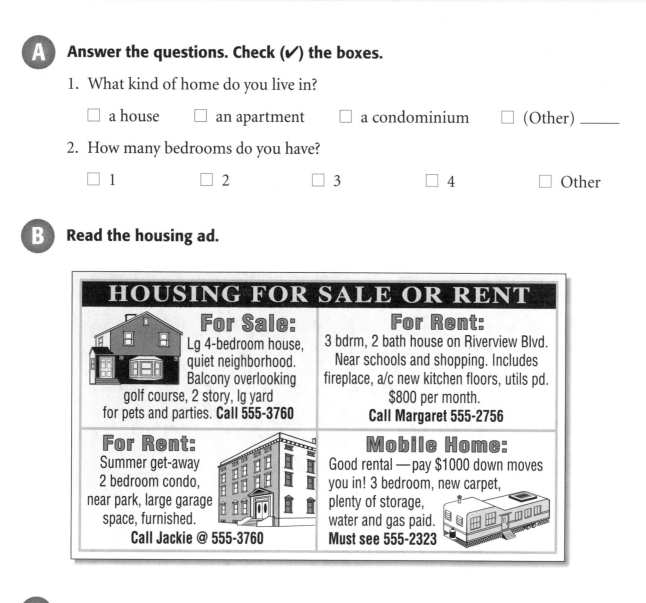

HOUSING FOR SALE OR RENT

For Sale:
Lg 4-bedroom house, quiet neighborhood. Balcony overlooking golf course, 2 story, lg yard for pets and parties. **Call 555-3760**

For Rent:
3 bdrm, 2 bath house on Riverview Blvd. Near schools and shopping. Includes fireplace, a/c new kitchen floors, utils pd. $800 per month.
Call Margaret 555-2756

For Rent:
Summer get-away 2 bedroom condo, near park, large garage space, furnished.
Call Jackie @ 555-3760

Mobile Home:
Good rental — pay $1000 down moves you in! 3 bedroom, new carpet, plenty of storage, water and gas paid.
Must see 555-2323

C **Complete the paragraph.**

Riverview is a beautiful community. We have a large _____-bedroom house

for sale right now. It has a _____ overlooking a golf course. We also have a

two-bedroom _____ near the _____. There is a mobile home

presently available with new _____ and plenty of storage. We also have

a three-bedroom house for rent. It is only _____ a month including

_____.

A Study the vocabulary.

The house is made of **bricks**.

Many houses in the U.S. are made of **wood**.

Some houses are built using **cement**.

The chair is made of **metal**.

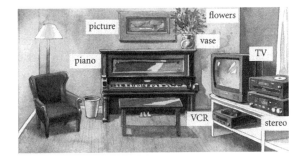

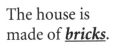

I need **furniture** for my living room.

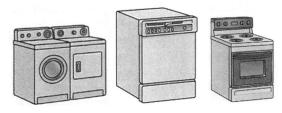

Dishwashers and stoves are **appliances**.

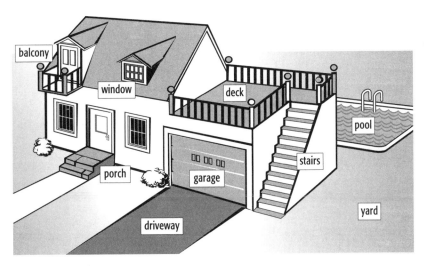

The house has a big **yard**.

There is a small **porch** at the front door.

The **balcony** is small.

The **driveway** is short.

They have a two-car **garage**.

There is a small **pool** in the backyard.

| brick | yard | sofa | | carpet | plastic | driveway | cement |
| pool | stove | dining table | | porch | wood | garage | |

Material	Inside a house	Outside a house
cement	*chair*	*balcony*

C You learned about adjectives in Unit 1. Adjectives describe nouns. Adjectives *always* come before the noun or after the verb *be*. Study the chart.

Adjective	Noun	Adjective after the noun	Adjective before the noun
big	yard	The **yard** is **big.**	The house has a **big yard.**
small	bedroom	The **bedrooms** are **small.**	The condo has **small bedrooms.**
nice	kitchen	The **kitchen** is **nice.**	The apartment has a **nice kitchen.**

 Rewrite the sentences.

1. The pool is new.

   The house has a new pool.

2. The balcony is old.

   _____

3. The yard is ugly.

   _____

4. The furniture is beautiful.

   _____

5. The bedrooms are small.

   _____

E **Write sentences about your home. Use adjectives and nouns from the box.**

Adjectives:	big	small	beautiful	old	new	ugly
Nouns:	furniture	kitchen	yard	appliances	house	

1. *I have a big house. There is a small balcony.*

2. _____

3. _____

4. _____

5. _____

6. _____

 F **Look at the pictures. Write sentences using *made of*.**

The vase is made of glass.

_____

_____

_____

 G **Write the nouns from this unit in your book. Look up the words below in a dictionary and add them to your notebook, too.**

plastic	window	roof	garden

► **PRE-READING**

A You are going to read about Kyung. He has to move to a new house. Look at the picture. What will be very important to Kyung as he looks for a new house? Check (✔) the boxes.

☐ 3 bathrooms

☐ a big yard

☐ 2 bedrooms

☐ a driveway

☐ a garage

☐ a pool

☐ near a park

☐ near schools

☐ near stores

B Look at the picture. Answer the questions.

1. What kind of house is this? _____

2. Where do you think it is? _____

3. What do you think it's made of? _____

C **Read about Kyung's move.**

Kyung's Mud House

Kyung is doing great at his job in Florida. His supervisor is very happy with his work. In fact, Kyung's boss[1] wants to give him a new job in the company. There is only one problem. He wants Kyung to move to New Mexico.

Kyung takes a trip to New Mexico to look for a house. He has an appointment with an agent from Wharton Realty. Kyung wants a four-bedroom house with a yard for a dog. He is very surprised because the first house they look at is made of mud.[2] The agent explains that the house is an adobe. Adobe houses are very popular in New Mexico. She shows him how it is cool[3] in the summer and warm[4] in the winter. They don't even need air conditioning!

Kyung likes the house. He especially likes the big yard and the beautiful plants all around. The rooms are large and the house has a beautiful kitchen. The windows are a little small but the agent explains that they are small so too much sun doesn't come into the house. Kyung calls home and tells his wife that he found the perfect house. He tells her "It has big rooms and a beautiful yard. Oh, and by the way, it's made of mud."

[1] **boss** – supervisor or leader at work
[2] **mud** – dirt and water
[3] **cool** – between cold and warm
[4] **warm** – between cool and hot

mud : bùn, sình
Adobe : gạch sống (đã nung)

▶ MAIN IDEA

D **Each paragraph has a sentence to prepare the reader for the paragraph. The sentence is called a *topic sentence*. It is usually the first sentence. Write the topic sentences.**

Paragraph 1: *Kyung is doing great at his job in Florida.*

Paragraph 2: _____

Paragraph 3: _____

▶ DETAILS

E **Kyung has a problem or a *conflict*. What is the problem or conflict in the story? Write the sentence that states the problem.**

_____

F **Read the sentences. Circle the correct usage.**

1. **mud**
   a. John walked into the house with *mud* on his feet.
   b. My favorite food in my house is *mud* with hot sauce.
   c. The *mud* in the kitchen was perfect.
2. **cool**
   a. The sun was overhead. It was 103 degrees. Maria was *cool* and happy.
   b. It wasn't hot or cold. The weather was *cool* with a little breeze.
   c. The family enjoyed the fireplace because when the fire was burning, it was very *cool*.

▶ EXTENSION

G **Talk to a partner. Do you think Kyung's wife was happy about Kyung's phone call?**

H **Ask four classmates these questions. Complete the chart.**

1. What kind of home do you live in?
2. What's your home like? Use adjectives.
3. What is your home made of?

Name	Question 1	Question 2	Question 3

WRITING CHALLENGE

▶ **PREPARING**

 Read about houses in Korea.

> ### Korean Houses
>
> April 15, 2006
>
> By Jiyoung Kim
>
> Houses in Korea are different from houses in the United States. Most houses are made of cement. Most people don't have carpets but they have other kinds of flooring. Most people have sofas in the living rooms, but some people prefer to sit on the floor. Most houses don't have grass in their yards. There are many beautiful houses in Korea.

 Write three ways houses in Korea are different from houses in the United States.

1. _____
2. _____
3. _____

C **What are houses like in your native country? Complete the chart.**

	Description of houses in _____
Materials	
Inside	
Outside	

D **Write four sentences about houses in your country.**

1. Most houses are made of _____

_____

2. Most houses have _____

_____

3. Most houses don't have _____

_____

4. Most people _____

_____

E **Every paragraph should have a topic sentence. Usually the topic sentence is the first sentence of the paragraph. The topic sentence gives the main idea of the paragraph. It prepares the reader for what comes next.**

> Korean Houses
>
> April 15, 2006
>
> By Jiyoung Kim
>
> Houses in Korea are different from houses in the United States. Most houses are made of cement. Most people don't have carpets, but they have other kinds of flooring. Most people have sofas in the living rooms, but some people prefer to sit on the floor. Most houses don't have grass in their yards. There are many beautiful houses in Korea.

topic sentence—main idea of the paragraph

Choose a topic sentence for your paragraph.

1. Houses in my country are different from houses in the United States.
2. Houses in my country are the same as houses in the United States.

 **Write a paragraph about homes in your native country.**

► **EDITING**

 Check your writing.

☐ Capital letters: My name is James. my name is james.

☐ Periods: I am from Argentina.

☐ Indent:

☐ Title, date, name

☐ Does it have a topic sentence?

Check a partner's writing.

☐ Capital letters: (M)y name is (J)ames. ~~m~~y name is ~~j~~ames.

☐ Periods: I am from Argentina⊙

☐ Indent: ⌐

☐ Title, date, name

☐ Does it have a topic sentence?

 Rewrite your paragraph on another sheet of paper.

 **▶ Community Challenge**

A **Find five people in your community who lived in another country. Make copies of the survey below. Complete the survey.**

Housing Survey

What's your name? _____

What's your nationality? _____

How long have you lived here? _____

Do you prefer living here or in another country? _____

Why? _____

What are houses made of in your country (wood, brick, cement, adobe, other)?

_____

 What did you find out? Present your findings to your classmates.

UNIT 5

Our Community

 GETTING READY

A Look at the picture.

B Describe this place. Check (✔) the boxes.

☐ It's a village.

☐ It's a city.

☐ It's hot.

☐ It's in the United States.

☐ It's in Mexico.

☐ People are having a good time.

A Answer the questions.

1. Where do you live? _____

2. Do tourists come to your city or town? Why? _____

B Read the city guide below.

Seaville
The Tiny Paradise!

SANDY BEACHES!

WATER SPORTS!

Visit the tiny town of Seaville where people of all ages can enjoy perfect weather year round. This is a beach paradise with fishing and every possible water sport. Lounge on the white sandy beaches under the warm sun and ocassional ocean breeze. Or swim in the cool waters and challenging surf. Rent a bike and ride along the bike path leading to Sunny Crest, the top of a small mountain overlooking all of Seaville.

THE AQUARIUM!

Visit the Aquarium which is open every day of the year.

For more information go to www.seaville.net

Don't forget! The Festival of the Sea August 15th

C Complete the paragraph about Felicia.

My name is Felicia and I live in Seaville, a _____ tiny r____ town _____ by _____ the ocean. I work in the Aquarium. It is open _____ every day _____ day. The weather in Seaville is _____ warm _____. On my day off, I like to go to the beach and read books. The sun is _____ hot _____ but the water is _____ cool _____. I have a bike and sometimes I ride to _____ funny crest _____. Every _____ year _____ we have a Festival. We celebrate the sea and all the animals. Seaville is a beautiful town. I am lucky to live here.

A Study the vocabulary.

I really like *festivals*! Spectators are *enjoying* the *parade*. There is a *fair* with a *ferris wheel*. The *clowns* and *magicians* are entertaining the children. People are *dancing* because there is a *band* playing.

Luisa is *getting married* today. It's her *wedding* day!

It is Ahmed's birthday *party* today.

My favorite *holiday* is New Year's. I like the *fireworks*.

B **Complete the paragraph with words from page 51. There can be more than one answer for some blank spaces.**

I am going to a _____ today. There will be a big

_____ down Main Street. The kids will love the funny

_____ and _____ . A famous

_____ will be playing rock music. I don't like

_____ so I will just watch. At night we will watch the

_____ . My dog doesn't like them because they are too loud.

C **You learned about nouns in Unit 2. *Pronouns* can be used in the place of nouns. Pronouns are *he, she, it,* and *they*. Study the chart.**

Subject: a noun	Subject: a pronoun
Alberto is having a birthday party.	**He** is having a birthday party.
Lien likes the parade.	**She** likes the parade.
The parade starts on First Street.	**It** starts on First Street.

D **Rewrite the sentences. Use pronouns in the second sentences.**

1. Mario dances in the parade. Mario has a lot of fun.

   _____

2. The party is for Jim. The party is to celebrate his wedding.

   _____

3. The two brothers went to the circus. The brothers laughed at the clowns.

   _____

4. The park is full of people having fun. The park is very noisy.

   _____

5. The fireworks are fun. The fireworks are very loud.

   _____

E Draw a line to match the words that are similar.

1. mall   a. town

2. team   b. shopping center

3. city   c. grassy place

4. park   d. group

5. stadium   e. arena

F Read. Find words that are similar to the words listed below.

Margie enjoys celebrations. She especially likes to eat cake and pie. Unfortunately Margie eats too much. She is 40 pounds overweight. She needs to go on a diet, but there is another party tomorrow. Margie will not stop!

enjoys   _likes_ _____

celebration _____

Margie _____

G Write the nouns from this unit in your notebook. Look up the words below in a dictionary and add them to your notebook, too.

picnic	circus	anniversary	concert

▶ PRE-READING

A What special holidays do you celebrate (for example, the 4th of July)?

_____

_____

B Have you been to a festival? What did you see? What did you do?
Check (✔) the boxes.

☐ a parade   ☐ clowns

☐ fireworks   ☐ magicians

☐ dancing   ☐ fairground rides

☐ music   ☐ Other: _____

☐ picnics   ☐ Other: _____

C The reading is about a special celebration in Santa Barbara in the United States.
What do you know about Santa Barbara?

1. Where is the city?

_____

2. What is the weather usually like?

_____

3. How many people live there?

_____

► READING

 Read about the Santa Barbara Solstice Parade and Festival.

A Celebration of Life

Santa Barbara is a good place to have a party. The weather is good all year. There is a beach and a beautiful downtown area. In June, Santa Barbara has a big parade and festival. It is called the Solstice Parade and Festival. The summer solstice is the longest day of the year and the first day of summer.

The Solstice Parade celebrates art and life. Over 1,000 people participate in the parade. They wear unusual costumes and masks. They sing and dance. The parade is full of music, dance, and color. The procession starts at 12:00 noon. It starts on the intersection of Cota and State Street and **runs**[1] along State Street for two miles. Over 100,000 **spectators**[2] line the route in front of stores and restaurants. The parade ends near the ocean at Alameda Park at 1:00.

The festival is fun for the whole family. There is live music, delicious food, and arts and crafts. There are also activities especially for children. Artists, musicians, and storytellers **entertain**.[3] The festival continues for seven hours. At the end of the day, people are tired but happy. They will enjoy Santa Barbara and the summer months to come.

[1] **runs** – goes
[2] **spectators** – people who watch
[3] **entertain** – put on a show for people

 Each paragraph has a sentence to prepare the reader for the paragraph. The sentence is called a *topic sentence*. Complete the topic sentences.

Paragraph 1: Santa Barbara is a _____

Paragraph 2: The Soltice Parade celebrates _____

Paragraph 3: The festival is _____

► **DETAILS**

 F **Answer the questions.**

1. How many people watch the parade? a. 1,000   b. 10,000   c. 100,000

2. What time does the parade start?   a. 12:00   b. 1:00   c. 10:00

3. Where does the parade end?   a. State Street   b. Cota Street   c. Alameda Park

4. How long does the festival last?   a. Seven hours   b. Ten hours   c. Twelve hours

G **Read the sentences. Circle the correct usage.**

1. **entertain**
   a. The movie star *entertains* the children in the hospital.
   b. The mother *entertains* the food for breakfast.
   c. When she is tired she *entertains* the television.

2. **spectator**
   a. I saw *spectators* dancing in the show.
   b. The *spectators* watched as the plane crashed.
   c. I went to the *spectators* for gas.

► **EXTENSION**

H **Ask four classmates these questions. Complete the chart.**

1. What kind of celebrations do you like?
2. When are the celebrations?
3. Where are the celebrations?

Name	Question 1	Question 2	Question 3

▶ WRITING CHALLENGE

▶ PREPARING

A Read about Ann's favorite celebration.

> *My Favorite Celebration*
>
> *June 15, 2006*
>
> *By Ann Gardener*
>
>   *My favorite celebration is the Fourth of July holiday. On the Fourth of July we celebrate American independence in the United States. There are fireworks, picnics, and family fun. I especially like spending time with my family. We play baseball and have a barbeque. The potato salad is delicious. At night we watch fireworks. The fourth of July is an all-day celebration.*

B Write four things that Ann does during the Fourth of July holiday.

1. _____
2. _____
3. _____
4. _____

C Make a list of celebrations you have in your native country.

_____

_____

_____

D What is your favorite celebration?

_____

E Write sentences about your favorite celebration.

1. When is the celebration?

_____

2. Where is the celebration?

_____

F Write four things that happen in the celebration.

_____

_____

_____

_____

G What is your favorite part of the celebration and why?

I especially like _____

because _____

H Look back at Ann's paragraph. Underline the topic sentence.

I You are going to write a paragraph about a celebration in your native country. Choose a topic sentence from the following list.

1. My favorite celebration in my country is _____.

2. I love celebrating _____ because I like

_____.

3. _____ is a great time of year.

4. Balloons, candy, and cake are special parts of birthday celebrations in my country.

▶ WRITING

J **Write a paragraph about your favorite celebration.**

▶ EDITING

A **Check your writing.**

☐ Capital letters: (M)y name is (J)ames. ~~my~~ name is ~~james~~.

☐ Periods: I am from Argentina.

☐ Title, date, name

☐ Indent: ⌐

☐ Does it have a topic sentence?

B Check a partner's writing.

☐ Capital letters: (M)y name is (J)ames. ~~my~~ name is ~~j~~ames.

☐ Periods: I am from Argentina.

☐ Title, date, name

☐ Indent: ⌒

☐ Does it have a topic sentence?

C Rewrite your paragraph on another sheet of paper.

▶ Community Challenge

What plans do you need to make to have a big celebration in your community? Plan a celebration and complete the information below.

Party Planning Guide

Type of party _____

Number of invitations _____

Day: _____   Time: _____

Guest list:

Food list:

Special entertainment:

_____

_____

_____

_____

UNIT 6 Health

▶ GETTING READY

 A **Look at the picture of Alexi.**

 B **Answer the questions.**

1. How old is Alexi?

_____

2. What is he doing?

_____

3. Do you think he is healthy?

_____

Answer the questions.

1. Are you healthy? _____

2. Do you exercise? _____

B **Read the health brochure.**

TOP 10 WAYS TO STAY HEALTHY!

1. Don't smoke. Smoking is the cause of over 400,000 deaths in the United States every year.

2. Don't drink. Over 100,000 deaths in the United States are alcohol related.

3. Exercise at least 30 minutes every day. This means to be physically active every day.

4. Eat a good diet. A good diet consists of plenty of vegetables and fruits, and don't forget the protein.

5. Eat small meals during the day. Eating one or two big meals a day is not as good as eating several small, healthy meals three or five times a day.

6. Get plenty of sleep. Most doctors now say that most people need to sleep at least 8 hours a night to stay healthy.

7. Reduce stress. To reduce stress, make sure you have a hobby or something fun to do regularly.

8. Go to the doctor at least once a year for a check-up. Doctors can help if you have a problem.

9. Follow the doctor's advice. Don't ignore warnings from the doctor.

10. Take vitamins every day. A multi-vitamin every day helps your body stay in balance.

 Complete the paragraph about good health practices.

Health goals are very personal. Doctors say some things are very important. For example, they say you should not drink too much or _____. They say that you should have a good diet and eat _____ meals. Sleep is also important. Doctors suggest that most people need _____ hours of sleep a night. Work is important, but too much work isn't. Doctors say that it is good to have a _____. Setting goals to be healthy is a good idea.

A Study the vocabulary.

Maria is _**healthy**_. She _**exercises**_ daily. She runs one mile every day.

She _**watches her diet**_. She eats a lot of fruits and vegetables.

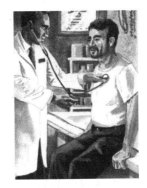

Gilberto _**gets a checkup**_ regularly, usually once a year.

I get lots of _**rest**_. I sleep from 10:00 P.M. to 6:00 A.M. every night.

Courtney is _**relaxed**_.

Minh is very _**busy**_. She has two jobs.

I _**smoke**_ cigarettes every day. It's _**unhealthy**_.

Nubar has a _**fast-paced**_ job. He has to work very fast to finish.

Amed's life is _**stressful**_. He is always _**worried**_ about something.

B **Complete the paragraph with words from page 63. There can be more than one answer for some blank spaces.**

The doctor says that I work too much and don't get enough _____.

I have a very _____ job. My work is _____

because I have so many responsibilities. I work all day and never see my family. I

_____ a lot about my family. The doctor also says that I need to

_____ more. He wants me to _____ my diet.

I will see him in six months for another _____.

C **Your lifestyle is the way you live your life. Some people have a healthy lifestyle, others have an unhealthy lifestyle. Complete the chart.**

Healthy lifestyle	Unhealthy lifestyle
exercising	smoking

D **Write sentences using the words in parentheses.**

1. The manager is very busy. (fast-paced)
   He has a fast-paced job. _____

2. The woman is healthy. (smoke)
   _____

3. I am worried about my job. (stressful)
   _____

4. I am not relaxed at work. (unhealthy)
   _____

E You learned in Unit 1 that adjectives go before the verb or after the *be* verb. Study the chart.

OK	Better
His life is stressful. It isn't healthy.	His stressful life isn't healthy.
The man is busy. He works twelve hours a day.	The busy man works twelve hours a day.

 F Follow the example in the chart above. Write one sentence for the two sentences.

1. His schedule is full. It is difficult for him.

   _____

2. We exercise in a gym. The gym is new.

   _____

3. The people are sick. They all smoke.

   _____

4. The job is fast-paced. It is for young people.

   _____

G Write the adjectives from this unit in your notebook. Look up the words below in a dictionary and add them to your notebook, too.

eventful	*demanding*	*rushed*	*challenging*

▶ **PRE-READING**

 A Look at the pictures. Match each picture to an emergency.

_____ a. is unconscious

_____ b. has chest pains

_____ c. has a broken arm

_____ d. has a stomachache

1.

3.

2.

4.

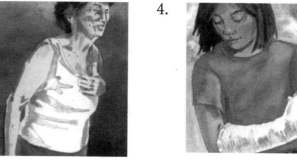

B The reading is about Alexi Tashkov. Alexi smokes cigarettes. How can smoking be bad for your health?

_____

_____

_____

C Do you smoke? Why or why not?

_____

D Alexi writes a letter to his friend Kasia in Russia. Why do you think he writes?

☐ He misses her.   ☐ He wants money.

☐ He has a problem.   ☐ He is getting married.

Read Alexi's letter.

September 15, 2005

Dear Kasia,

How are you? I'm sorry I haven't written you for a long time. I had some health problems. I didn't write to you because I didn't want you to worry.

I had a very bad habit. I started smoking when I came to the United States. I smoked one pack of cigarettes a day. I am young and I didn't think it was a problem. I thought I would quit smoking in ten years. I was tired a lot and my teacher at school said that I should go to the doctor. I didn't go because I was so busy. I have a stressful job.

I finally went to the doctor and he told me to stop smoking. I didn't stop. I exercised every day, I played soccer on the weekend, and I never had trouble **breathing**[1], so I didn't listen to the doctor. I should have listened to him. I had a small heart attack. I'm fine now, so don't worry about me. In fact, I feel better than ever, and I am taking care of myself.

I stopped smoking about three months ago after my heart attack. I have to take medicine every day. I have to exercise regularly and watch my diet. The doctor said that my heart is strong now and that I should be fine. I will slow down from now on and try to enjoy life.

I promise that I will be careful and I will never smoke again. I want to visit you soon. Do you think I can visit you in Moscow in the summer? I hope to see you soon.

Best,

Alexi

[1] **breathing** – taking air into the lungs

F A *summary* is a short description of a longer story or passage. Read the three summaries below. Which one is a good summary of Alexi's letter to his friend? Why is he writing?

1. Alexi writes that he had a heart attack, but now he is fine.
2. Alexi writes that he misses his friend and wants to visit her in Moscow.
3. Alexi writes to tell his friend about the medicine he is taking.

▶ DETAILS

G Answer the questions.

1. When did Alexi stop smoking?
   a. when he was feeling tired a lot
   b. after the doctor told him to
   c. after he had a heart attack

2. What life changes does he have to make?

   _____

   _____

▶ EXTENSION

H Ask four classmates these questions. Complete the chart.

1. How much do you exercise every day?
2. Do you have any unhealthy habits? What is one?
3. Do you have many friends who smoke? How many?

Name	Question 1	Question 2	Question 3

▶ WRITING CHALLENGE

▶ PREPARING

A Read Patty's letter.

> September 10, 2005
>
> Dear Mom,
>
> How are you? I am fine. I am healthy and happy. I miss you. I want to tell you about life in the United States.
>
> The lifestyle here is very different. Everyone here is very busy. Many people work ten or twelve hours a day. I think everyone is in a hurry. I am, too. I work nights all week from 10:00 P.M. to 7:00 A.M. I go to school during the day to learn English. I spend every free minute with my family. The babies and my husband are fine. We are happy, but very busy.
>
> Please write to me soon.
>
> Love,
>
> Patty

B Look at Patty's first paragraph. In a letter, you should write the purpose of the letter (why you are writing) at the beginning. <u>Underline</u> the sentence Patty uses to state the purpose of the letter.

You are going to write a letter. The purpose of this letter is *"I want to tell you about life in the United States."*

C Look at Patty's second paragraph. <u>Underline</u> the topic sentence.
What topic sentence do you want to use for the second paragraph of your letter?

    a. The lifestyle here is very different.
    b. My life here is the same as in our country.
    c. I am very busy every day here.
    d. I am bored. There isn't a lot to do.
    e. Other _____

D Make a list of family members who don't live in the same country as you do now.

_____

_____

E Who do you want to write to?

_____

F Write sentences describing your schedule. What do you do every day?

In the morning, I _____

In the afternoon, I _____

In the evening, I _____

On the weekends, I _____

G Answer the questions about your lifestyle.

1. Are you busy or not very busy?

_____

2. How is your lifestyle different from others?

_____

_____

3. Do you think you are healthy? Why or why not?

_____

_____

► **WRITING**

 Write a letter.

► **EDITING**

I **Check your writing.**

☐ Capital letters: Ⓜy name is Ⓙames. ~~m~~y name is ~~j~~ames.

☐ Periods: I am from Argentina⊙

☐ Indent: ⌐

☐ Does it express the purpose of the letter?

☐ Does it have a topic sentence?

J **Check a partner's writing.**

☐ Capital letters: Ⓜy name is Ⓙames. ~~m~~y name is ~~j~~ames.

☐ Periods: I am from Argentina⊙

☐ Indent: ⌐

☐ Does it express the purpose of the letter?

☐ Does it have a topic sentence?

 Rewrite your letter on another sheet of paper and send it.

A Take a poll. Find out how many people in your community exercise. Ask 20 people. Complete the chart.

Do you . . . ?					
exercise-walk	swim	ride a bike	run	play soccer	go to the gym

B Make a bar graph.

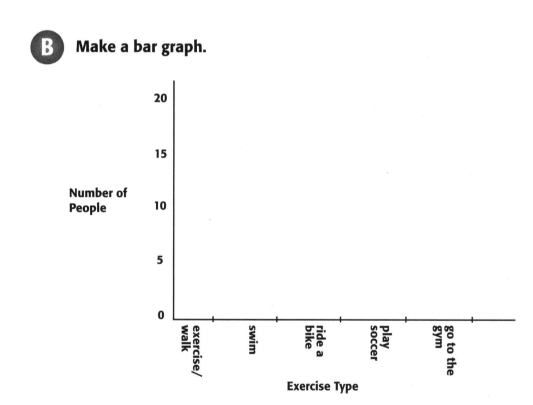

C Report your findings to the class.

UNIT 7

Work, Work, Work

▶ GETTING READY

 A Look at the picture of Dalva.

 B Ask and answer. Check (✓) the boxes.

1. What is Dalva's job?

   ☐ she's an assistant   ☐ she's a mechanic

2. Where does she work?

   ☐ at home   ☐ in an office

3. Do you think she likes her job?

   ☐ yes   ☐ no

► **READING CHALLENGE 1**

 Answer the questions.

1. Do you have a job? If so, what is your job?

_____

2. Do you like your job? Why?

_____

 Read the classifieds.

DAILY NEWS CLASSIFIED ADS

Cashier Needed
no exp. OK, FT, $8.50
an hour, Alton Market.
Call 555-3745

Hotel Manager
5 years experience,
apply on-site,
FT w/benefits, 401k,
2923 Acorn Blvd.
Hotel Stratton

Gardener Wanted
P/T, experience a must,
full benefits, large
estate in Wilshire area.
Call 555-3765

Homecare Nurses
Live in, take care of two
seniors, prepare meals,
keep track of medicine
etc. Reasonable pay plan.
Call 555-6565

Police Officers
Apply today for a
rewarding career.
We train. Call 555-9123.

Mechanics Needed
Jif Tune-Ups—certified
mechanics only please.
$14.50 to start. Benefits,
vacation, retirement.
Call 555-4123

C **Complete the paragraph about Lien and her store. Circle your answers.**

The gardener position is the only full-time/part-time position open. They want/don't want

someone with experience. Jif Tune-Ups needs certified managers/mechanics. The position

includes/doesn't include benefits. The hotel needs a new assistant/manager with five/two years

experience. The supermarket needs cashiers. They pay $8.50/$14.50 an hour.

A Study the <u>underlined</u> words. Look up the words you don't know in a dictionary.

☐ I <u>follow instructions</u> well.

☐ My wife <u>works hard</u>.

☐ Manuel has a <u>positive attitude</u>.

☐ I am <u>sociable</u>.

☐ Katerina is always <u>on time</u>.

☐ My boss makes <u>difficult decisions</u>.

☐ My manager is very <u>knowledgeable</u>.

☐ I <u>help</u> others at work.

B Write the letter of the definition next to the vocabulary word.

_____ 1. Someone who <u>follows instructions</u>

_____ 2. Someone who has a <u>positive attitude</u>

_____ 3. Someone who <u>works hard</u>

_____ 4. Someone who is <u>on time</u>

_____ 5. Someone who is <u>knowledgeable</u>

_____ 6. Someone who <u>is helpful</u>

_____ 7. Someone who <u>makes decisions</u>

_____ 8. Someone who <u>is sociable</u>

a. talks to people easily

b. usually comes to work at the right time

c. listens to his/her boss

d. is excited to do something

e. helps other people

f. understands a lot about something

g. works all day

h. decides what to do

C Complete the paragraph with words from Exercise A.

Dalva is a good worker. She likes to do a good job. She works very _____,

but she sometimes is not very _____. Dalva has a _____

attitude, and she always comes to work _____. She also likes

to _____ others. In this job, it is very important to make

_____. Dalva is a wonderful employee.

D Look at the photos. What qualities do you think are most important for these jobs?

_____   _____   _____

_____   _____   _____

_____   _____   _____

E Conjunctions are words that connect two sentences together. Use _and_ to connect two sentences that have similar ideas. Use _but_ to connect sentences that are opposite or very different. Study the chart.

and	
Dalva has a good attitude.	Dalva always comes to work on time.
Dalva has a good attitude, **and** she always comes to work on time.	

but	
Dalva works hard.	Dalva is not very organized.
Dalva works hard, **but** she is not very organized.	

F Complete the sentences with _but_ or _and._

1. Gilberto is organized, _____ he makes good decisions.

2. Marie is on-time, _____ she doesn't follow instructions.

3. Orlando learns quickly, _____ he doesn't work hard.

4. Sara follows instructions, _____ she has a positive attitude.

5. Ana doesn't make decisions, _____ she helps others.

6. Alexi isn't knowledgeable, _____ he learns quickly.

G You learned to use *because* in Unit 2. Use *because* to connect two complete sentences also, but don't use commas. Write one sentence for the two sentences. Use *because.*

1. Dalva is a good employee. She works very hard.

   Dalva is a good employee because she works very hard.

2. They are successful. They have good attitudes.

   _____

3. We are team players. It is the best way to work.

   _____

4. I make decisions. No other people will make them.

   _____

5. He learns quickly. He listens carefully.

   _____

H Write five sentences about you and your job. Use *and*, *but*, and *because.*

1. _____

2. _____

3. _____

4. _____

5. _____

I Write the words from this unit in your notebook. Look up the words below in a dictionary and add them to your notebook, too.

punctual	*cheerful*	*cooperative*	*successful*

▶ **PRE-READING**

A **What do you do? Check (✓) the boxes.**

☐ doctor   ☐ student   ☐ office assistant

☐ mechanic   ☐ cashier   ☐ custodian

☐ engineer   ☐ delivery person   ☐ Other: _____

☐ homemaker   ☐ server

B **What do you do in your job? Make a list.**

1. *I type letters.* _____

2. _____

3. _____

4. _____

5. _____

6. _____

7. _____

C **You are going to read Dalva's evaluation report. She is an assistant manager at a hotel. What skills or qualities do you need for that job? Check (✓) the boxes.**

☐ speak other languages   ☐ organize schedules

☐ use a computer   ☐ fix cars

☐ use a cash register   ☐ clean offices

☐ manage people   ☐ protect people

☐ drive a truck   ☐ positive attitude

READING

 D **Read the evaluation report.**

Employee Evaluation Report

Employee name: Dalva Mendez
Position: Assistant Manager
Supervisor: Patricia Macias, General Manager

This report evaluates Dalva Mendez's job performance as an Assistant Manager. Dalva is a very hard worker. She works well with other employees, and she learns quickly. She always has a positive attitude.

Dalva came to Fairview in December 2001. We **hired**[1] her as an administrative assistant. She took English classes in the morning and worked for us in the evening. In November 2002, she wanted to leave because she had a job offer from another company. I promoted Dalva to desk clerk because I didn't want her to leave. She liked her job because she could speak to customers. She speaks Spanish, French, and Portuguese, as well as English.

In July 2003, we needed a new assistant manager. Dalva was the perfect candidate. I promoted her again. She managed the desk clerks and prepared schedules. She has many ideas on making Fairview Hotel the best hotel in the county. I am happy to listen to her ideas.

Dalva is an excellent employee. She has contributed to our business in many ways, including working late and on weekends. She is one of the best employees at the hotel.

---

[1] **hired** – gave a job to

E **Each paragraph has a different idea. Write the number of the paragraph.**

Paragraph number	Main idea
	Conclusion
	Purpose of the report
	Dalva's present job
	Dalva's first jobs at Fairview Hotel

▶ **DETAILS**

F **Answer the questions. Write complete sentences.**

1. What four qualities does Dalva have?

   _____

   _____

   _____

   _____

2. What languages can she speak? _____

3. What is Dalva's current job? _____

G **Read the sentences. Choose the correct meaning of the boldfaced words.**

1. She has **contributed** to our business in many ways, including working late
   and on weekends.
   Contribute means _____.

   a. to give (money, one's time, etc.)
   b. to participate positively in something

2. I **promoted** Dalva to a desk clerk because I didn't want her to leave.
   Promote means _____.

   a. to advance in rank, give someone a better job
   b. to make known to the public, advertise goods and services

▶ **EXTENSION**

H **Ask four classmates these questions. Complete the chart.**

1. How long have you worked at your present job?
2. What jobs have you had?
3. What job did you like the best?

Name	Question 1	Question 2	Question 3

► **PREPARING**

A Dalva is applying for a new job. Read Dalva's job application letter.

January 28, 2005

345 E. Birch Avenue
San Francisco, CA

Ms. Lynette Applebee
2345 W. Counter Blvd.
Needlewood, NM.

Dear Ms. Applebee:

Please consider my application for the hotel manager position. I think that I could do a good job in this position.

I have three years of experience in the hotel business. I can type, and I can speak English and Spanish. I can work every weekday, Monday through Friday. I am available between 7:00 A.M. and 6:00 P.M.

I am a good worker. I am very enthusiastic, and I always work well in a team.

I look forward to hearing from you soon.

Sincerely,
Dalva Mendez
Dalva Mendez

B Answer the questions. Circle *True* or *False*.

1. Dalva wants the hotel manager job.   True   False

2. She has two years experience.   True   False

3. She can't type.   True   False

4. She can work on Saturdays.   True   False

C Choose one of the jobs that you like from the ad on page 74. You are going to write a letter of application for this job. What skills do you need for this job? Check (✓) the boxes.

☐ speak other languages
☐ use a computer
☐ use a cash register
☐ drive a truck

☐ fix cars
☐ clean offices
☐ protect people

D How much experience do you need for this job? Check (✓) the boxes.

☐ no experience
☐ 6 months experience
☐ 1 year experience

☐ 2 to 3 years experience
☐ 5 years experience

E Check (✓) the qualities that describe you.

☐ I am enthusiastic.
☐ I am always on time.
☐ I follow instructions well.

☐ I help others.
☐ I am friendly.
☐ I have a good attitude.

☐ I make decisions.
☐ I am helpful.

F An application letter is a business letter. Study the format of a business letter.

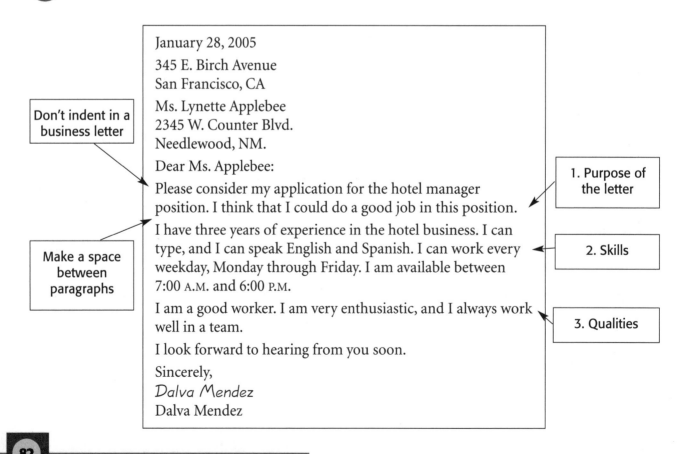

January 28, 2005
345 E. Birch Avenue
San Francisco, CA

Ms. Lynette Applebee
2345 W. Counter Blvd.
Needlewood, NM.

Dear Ms. Applebee:

Please consider my application for the hotel manager position. I think that I could do a good job in this position.

I have three years of experience in the hotel business. I can type, and I can speak English and Spanish. I can work every weekday, Monday through Friday. I am available between 7:00 A.M. and 6:00 P.M.

I am a good worker. I am very enthusiastic, and I always work well in a team.

I look forward to hearing from you soon.

Sincerely,
Dalva Mendez
Dalva Mendez

Don't indent in a business letter

Make a space between paragraphs

1. Purpose of the letter

2. Skills

3. Qualities

► WRITING

G Write a letter of application. Use the model on page 81.

EDITING

 Check your writing.

- ☐ Capital letters
- ☐ Periods
- ☐ Good sentences (subject/verb)
- ☐ No indents
- ☐ Space between each paragraph
- ☐ 3 paragraphs (purpose, qualifications, qualities)

 Check a partner's writing.

- ☐ Capital letters
- ☐ Periods
- ☐ Good sentences (subject/verb)
- ☐ No indents
- ☐ Space between each paragraph
- ☐ 3 paragraphs (purpose, qualifications, qualities)

 Rewrite your letter on another sheet of paper and send it.

▶ Community Challenge

 Find a newspaper and look for a job. Get an application. Complete the application and return it with a typed letter. Ask for an interview.

 Practice interviewing skills with people in your community.

Goals and Lifelong Learning

▶ GETTING READY

A Look at the picture of Marie.

B Answer the questions.

1. What is the name of her school?

   _____

2. What is the man giving to Marie?

   _____

3. What is this ceremony called?

   _____

A **Answer the questions.**

1. What is the name of your school? _____

2. What time do you go to school? _____

B **Read the page from a class schedule.**

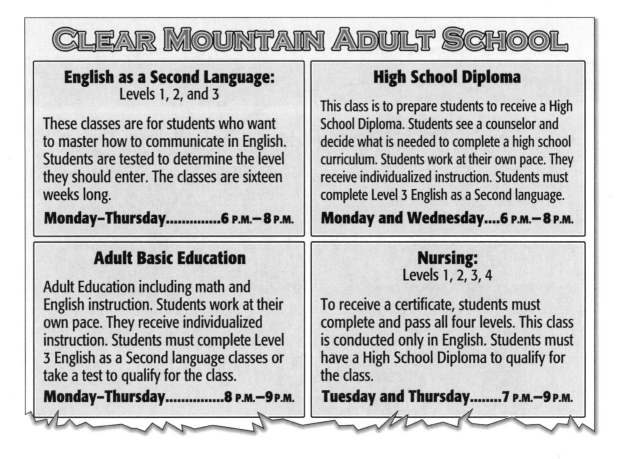

CLEAR MOUNTAIN ADULT SCHOOL

English as a Second Language:
Levels 1, 2, and 3

These classes are for students who want to master how to communicate in English. Students are tested to determine the level they should enter. The classes are sixteen weeks long.

Monday–Thursday..............6 P.M.–8 P.M.

High School Diploma

This class is to prepare students to receive a High School Diploma. Students see a counselor and decide what is needed to complete a high school curriculum. Students work at their own pace. They receive individualized instruction. Students must complete Level 3 English as a Second language.

Monday and Wednesday....6 P.M.–8 P.M.

Adult Basic Education

Adult Education including math and English instruction. Students work at their own pace. They receive individualized instruction. Students must complete Level 3 English as a Second language classes or take a test to qualify for the class.

Monday–Thursday...............8 P.M.–9 P.M.

Nursing:
Levels 1, 2, 3, 4

To receive a certificate, students must complete and pass all four levels. This class is conducted only in English. Students must have a High School Diploma to qualify for the class.

Tuesday and Thursday........7 P.M.–9 P.M.

C **Complete the paragraph about Marie.**

My name is Marie Escobar. I go to Clear Mountain _____. My goal is to be a nurse. I study Level 3 English. The class meets _____ days a week. When I finish that course I need to get a high school _____. When I get my diploma, I want to take nursing classes to receive a _____. I will work hard to reach my goal.

A Look at the words and pictures.

Marie **_brainstormed_** all the things she could do in the future.

Marie **_listed_** all of her goals.

Marie **_selected_** the most important goal.

I **_displayed_** my goal on the fridge.

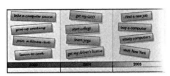

I **_made a plan_** for my goals.

Marie **_reached_** her goal. She got a diploma.

B Complete the paragraph with words from Exercise A.

Marie wanted to think about her work goals. First she _____ all the ideas she has. She _____ these ideas on a piece of paper. Then she _____ the one she liked best. Next she wrote the goal on a piece of paper, and _____ it on the refrigerator where she saw it every day. Finally, she _____ for each year. Marie hoped to _____ her goal in three years.

C Complete the chart with words from the box.

| brainstorm | list | select | display | plan | reach |

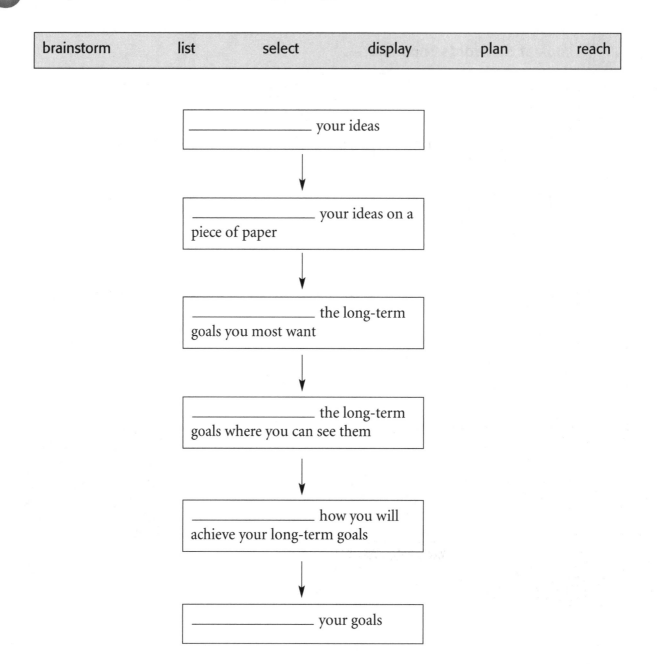

_____ your ideas

↓

_____ your ideas on a piece of paper

↓

_____ the long-term goals you most want

↓

_____ the long-term goals where you can see them

↓

_____ how you will achieve your long-term goals

↓

_____ your goals

D *Synonyms* are words that mean the same. For example, "like" and "enjoy" are synonyms. Draw a line to match the synonyms.

1. reach   a. post

2. display   b. think

3. brainstorm   c. choose

4. select   d. accomplish

E **Rewrite the second sentences below and replace the <u>underlined</u> word.**

1. Marie thought of some goals. She <u>thought of</u> all the ideas and put them on a piece of paper.

   _____

2. Marie chose one or two of the best ideas. She <u>chose</u> the goals by deciding which ones were most important to her.

   _____

3. Marie posted the goals on the refrigerator and worked on them every day. She remembered them because they were <u>posted</u> where she could see them.

   _____

4. Marie accomplished many goals. She <u>accomplished</u> the goals by working on them with every opportunity she had.

   _____

F *Transition words* **help the reader understand the order of ideas. Study the transition words. Then look back at Marie's goals in Exercise B. Circle all the transition words.**

first	next	then	finally

G **Write the transition words from Exercise F.**

Mario wants to start his own business.
_____ he needs to go to Adult School.
_____ he wants to get a part-time job in an automobile shop. _____ he wants to go to community college and study auto mechanics and accounting. _____, he will be able to start his own auto repair business.

H **Write the verbs from this unit in your notebook.**

▶ **PRE-READING**

A Check (✔) all the long-term goals you have.

☐ I want to get a job. ☐ I want to move. ☐ I want to finish school.

☐ I want a better job. ☐ I want to buy a house. ☐ I want to learn English better.

☐ I want to keep my job. ☐ I want to get married. ☐ I want to go to college.

☐ I want to make a lot of money. ☐ I want children. ☐ I want a high school diploma.

☐ I want to travel to many countries. ☐ I want to be healthier. ☐ I want a GED.

☐ Other: _____ ☐ Other: _____ ☐ Other: _____

B Talk to you partner. Complete the chart.

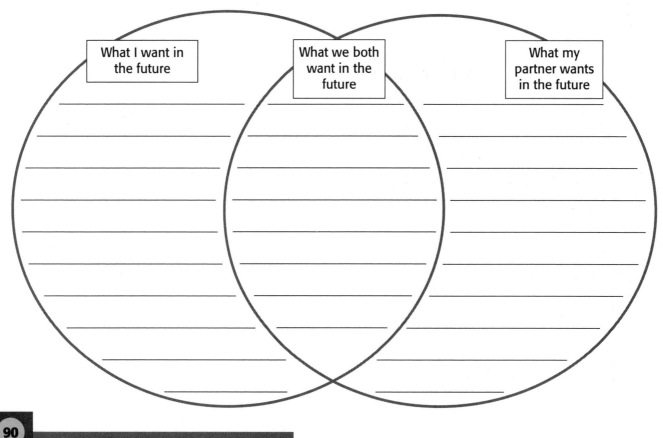

What I want in the future

What we both want in the future

What my partner wants in the future

► READING

Read about goals.

> Many successful people *set*[1] goals. Goals are part of every successful business. At the beginning of each year, many people set personal goals, called New Year resolutions. Personal goals can be about your family, your education, or your work.
>
> There are several steps to setting your long-term goals. First brainstorm your ideas. Where do you want to be in five or ten years? Write down your long-term goals. Do you want to get a degree? Do you want to be a manager? Do you want to buy a house? It is important that you write down your ideas. List them on a computer and display them where you will see them every day. For example, you *might*[2] put them on the refrigerator.
>
> Now that you have set your long-term goals, it is time to plan what you need to do every day to reach those goals. Short-term goals can be daily, weekly, or even monthly goals. For example, if you have a long-term goal to lose thirty-five pounds in one year, you might decide to lose three pounds a month. What do you need to do to lose three pounds this month? You might make daily goals for changing your eating habits, or you might have a goal to study how to do it. You could go to a health club and set goals with them. *Again,*[3] write down your goals and read them every day so you can focus on them.
>
> Make sure you set personal goals you can reach. Some people make the same resolutions every year and never reach them because they don't make short-term goals. Sometimes the goals are not realistic. Reach the easier short-term goals and you will find success in the long term and in life.

[1] **set** – make
[2] **might** – maybe
[3] **again** – one more time

► MAIN IDEAS

What is a good title for this article?

_____

Write the topic sentences.

Paragraph 1: _Many successful people set goals._____

Paragraph 2: _____

Paragraph 3: _____

Paragraph 4: _____

▶ DETAILS

 Answer these questions.

1. Write three kinds of personal goals.

_____

_____

_____

2. Is losing thirty pounds a year a short-term or long-term goal?

_____

3. What are two words for "make"?

_____   _____

 What dictionary definition from the *Basic Newbury House Dictionary of American English* is right for the boldfaced words?

1. For example, if you have a long-term goal to lose thirty-five pounds in one year, you might **decide** to lose three pounds a month.
   Decide means _____.
   a. to make a choice
   b. to bring to a certain end

2. Again, write your goals down and read them every day so you can **focus** on them.
   Focus means _____.
   a. to change in order to get a clear picture
   b. to centers one's attention on something

▶ EXTENSION

 Ask four classmates these questions. Complete the chart.

1. Do you have long-term goals?
2. What are your long-term goals?

Name	Question 1	Question 2

▶ **PREPARING**

A Read about Ahmed's goals.

> **My Goals**
>
> January 15, 2005
>
> By Ahmed Kalim
>
>
> My long-term goal is to get a high school diploma. First I need to learn English. I want to learn English fast. I'm going to come to school every day, listen carefully, and practice a lot. Then I need to talk to a counselor. He can help me decide what classes to take. Finally, I can take high school classes. I hope I can get my high school diploma soon, so I can help my family with a better job.

B Complete the chart about Ahmed.

Long-term goal	Short-term goals
to get a high school diploma	

You are going to write about your goals. Choose two long-term goals. Make a list of short-term goals to reach the long-term ones.

Long-term goal 1	Short-term goals

Long-term goal 2	Short-term goals

 Choose a topic sentence.

1. I have many goals, but one is very important to me.

2. My long-term goal is to _____.

3. I have one long-term goal for the next five years.

4. You need English to go to a university, and I plan to speak good English in two years.

5. I need a high school diploma so I can get a good job.

6. Other: _____

► **WRITING**

 **Write a paragraph about your goals.**

► **EDITING**

 Check your writing.

☐ Capital letters: My name is James. my name is james.

☐ Periods: I am from Argentina.

☐ Indent: ⌐

☐ Does it have a topic sentence?

Check a partner's writing.

☐ Capital letters: (M)y name is (J)ames. ~~m~~y name is ~~j~~ames.

☐ Periods: I am from Argentina.

☐ Indent: ⌐

☐ Does it have a topic sentence?

 Rewrite your paragraph on another sheet of paper.

▶ Community Challenge

 Talk to three people in the community who are successful. Ask them if they set goals. Ask them what goals they set and how they accomplished them.

1. Name: _____

   Profession: _____

   Goals now: _____

   Goals five years ago: _____

   Goals ten years ago: _____

2. Name: _____

   Profession: _____

   Goals now: _____

   Goals five years ago: _____

   Goals ten years ago: _____

3. Name: _____

   Profession: _____

   Goals now: _____

   Goals five years ago: _____

   Goals ten years ago: _____

APPENDIX

▶ VOCABULARY LIST

Unit 1
tall
short
thin
heavy
handsome
beautiful
bald
shy
smart
talkative
friendly
hardworking
happy
nervous
tired

Unit 2
regular price
sales price
sale
save
customer
salesperson
coupon
sales tax
total
fitting room

Unit 3
tablespoon
teaspoon
pound
cup
mix
boil
add
chop
cook
peel
sweet
salty
hot
spicy
delicious

Unit 4
bricks
wood
cement
metal
furniture
appliances
yard
porch
balcony
driveway
garage
pool

Unit 5
festivals
enjoying
parade
fair
ferris wheel
clowns
magicians
dancing
bad
getting married
wedding
party
holiday
fireworks

Unit 6
healthy
exercise
watch someone's diet
get a checkup
rest
relaxed
busy
smoke
unhealthy
fast-paced
stressful
worried

Unit 7
follow instructions
positive attitude
on-time
helpful
knowledgeable
work hard
sociable
difficult decisions
helpful

Unit 8
brainstormed
listed
selected
displayed
plan
reached
first
next
then
finally

▶ IRREGULAR VERB FORMS

be	was	**hear**	heard
become	became	**hide**	hid
begin	began	**hit**	hit
blow	blew	**keep**	kept
break	broke	**know**	knew
bring	brought	**lead**	led
build	built	**leave**	left
buy	bought	**lose**	lost
catch	caught	**make**	made
choose	chose	**meet**	met
come	came	**pay**	paid
cut	cut	**put**	put
do	did	**run**	ran
drink	drank	**say**	said
drive	drove	**see**	saw
eat	ate	**send**	sent
fall	fell	**sleep**	slept
feel	felt	**speak**	spoke
fight	fought	**spend**	spent
find	found	**take**	took
fly	flew	**teach**	taught
forget	forgot	**tell**	told
get	got	**think**	thought
give	gave	**understand**	understood
go	went	**wear**	wore
grow	grew	**win**	won
have	had	**write**	wrote

▶ USEFUL WORDS

Cardinal numbers

1	one
2	two
3	three
4	four
5	five
6	six
7	seven
8	eight
9	nine
10	ten
11	eleven
12	twelve
13	thirteen
14	fourteen
15	fifteen
16	sixteen
17	seventeen
18	eighteen
19	nineteen
20	twenty
21	twenty-one
30	thirty
40	forty
50	fifty
60	sixty
70	seventy
80	eighty
90	ninety
100	one hundred
1000	one thousand
10,000	ten thousand
100,000	one hundred thousand
1,000,000	one million

Ordinal numbers

first	1st
second	2nd
third	3rd
fourth	4th
fifth	5th
sixth	6th
seventh	7th
eighth	8th
ninth	9th
tenth	10th
eleventh	11th
twelfth	12th
thirteenth	13th
fourteenth	14th
fifteenth	15th
sixteenth	16th
seventeenth	17th
eighteenth	18th
nineteenth	19th
twentieth	20th
twenty-first	21st

Days of the week

Sunday
Monday
Tuesday
Wednesday
Thursday
Friday
Saturday

Seasons

winter
spring
summer
fall

Months of the year

January
February
March
April
May
June
July
August
September
October
November
December

Write the date

April 5, 2004 = 4/ 5/ 04

Temperature chart

Degrees Celsius (°C) and
Degrees Fahrenheit (°F)

100°C	212°F
30°C	86°F
25°C	77°F
20°C	68°F
15°C	59°F
10°C	50°F
5°C	41°F
0°C	32°F
−5°C	23°F

Weights and measures

Weight:
1 pound (lb.) = 453.6 grams (g)
16 ounces (oz.) = 1 pound (lb.)
1 pound (lb.) = .45 kilogram (kg)

Liquid or Volume:
1 cup (c.) = .24 liter (l)
2 cups (c.) = 1 pint (pt.)
2 pints = 1 quart (qt.)
4 quarts = 1 gallon (gal.)
1 gallon (gal.) = 3.78 liters (l)

Length:
1 inch (in. or ″) = 2.54 centimeters (cm)
1 foot (ft. or ′) = .3048 meters (m)
12 inches (12″) = 1 foot (1′)
1 yard (yd.) = 3 feet (3′) or 0.9144 meters (m)
1 mile (mi.) = 1609.34 meters (m) or 1.609 kilometers (km)

Time:
60 seconds = 1 minute
60 minutes = 1 hour
24 hours = 1 day
28–31 days = 1 month
12 months = 1 year

MAP OF THE UNITED STATES

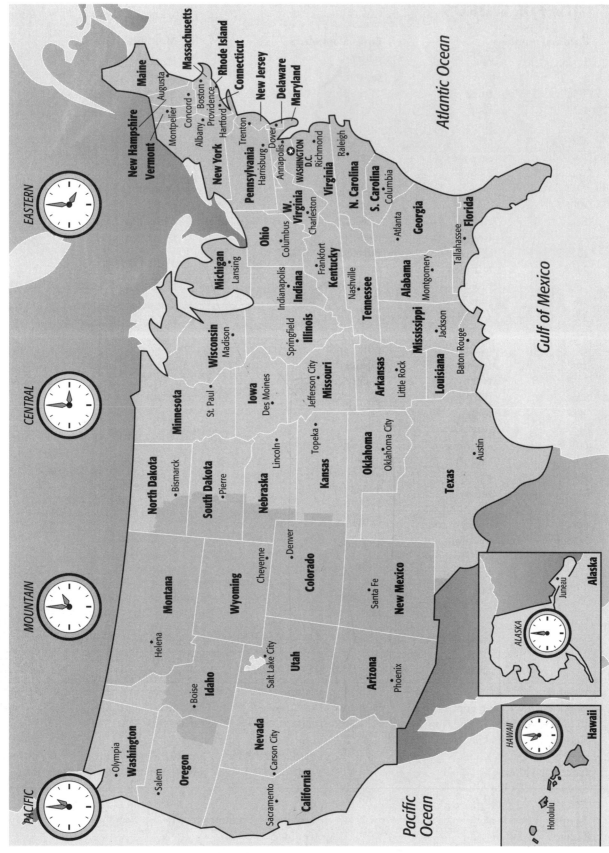

PACIFIC

MOUNTAIN

CENTRAL

EASTERN

Pacific Ocean

Atlantic Ocean

Gulf of Mexico

Washington
• Olympia
• Salem
Oregon

Nevada
• Carson City

California
• Sacramento

Idaho
• Boise

Montana
• Helena

Utah
• Salt Lake City

Wyoming
• Cheyenne

Colorado
• Denver

Arizona
• Phoenix

New Mexico
• Santa Fe

North Dakota
• Bismarck

South Dakota
• Pierre

Nebraska
• Lincoln

Kansas
• Topeka

Oklahoma
• Oklahoma City

Texas
• Austin

Minnesota
• St. Paul

Iowa
• Des Moines

Missouri
• Jefferson City

Arkansas
• Little Rock

Louisiana
• Baton Rouge

Wisconsin
• Madison

Illinois
• Springfield

Michigan
• Lansing

Indiana
• Indianapolis

Ohio
• Columbus

Kentucky
• Frankfort

Tennessee
• Nashville

Mississippi
• Jackson

Alabama
• Montgomery

Georgia
• Atlanta

Florida
• Tallahassee

S. Carolina
• Columbia

N. Carolina
• Raleigh

Virginia
• Richmond

W. Virginia
• Charleston

Pennsylvania
• Harrisburg

New York
• Albany

Maine
• Augusta

Vermont
• Montpelier

New Hampshire
• Concord

Massachusetts
• Boston

Rhode Island
• Providence

Connecticut
• Hartford

New Jersey
• Trenton

Delaware
• Dover

Maryland
• Annapolis

WASHINGTON D.C.

ALASKA
Alaska
• Juneau

HAWAII
Hawaii
• Honolulu